FACT FINDERS

Educational adviser: Arthur Razzell

Warships

Hugh Gregor

Illustrated by Richard Hook,
Dick Eastland and Eric Jewell Associates
Designed by Faulkner/Marks Partnership

Silver Burdett Company

Published in the United
Stated by Silver Burdett
Company, Morristown, N.J.
1978 Printing

ISBN 0-382-06242-6

Library of Congress
Catalog Card No. 78-64660

Warships

The First Warships

The first sea-going ships were called galleys. The first galleys were trading ships. Later, galleys were also built as warships.

This Greek galley was called a trireme. It carried 170 men to work the oars. It has a heavy ram below water level. This was used to sink enemy ships.

Greek trireme

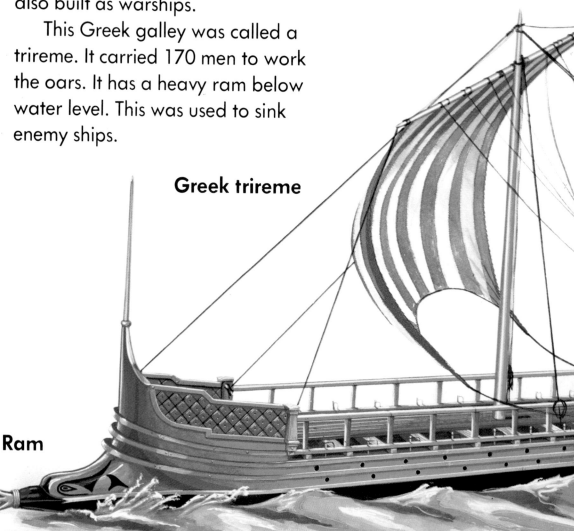

Ram

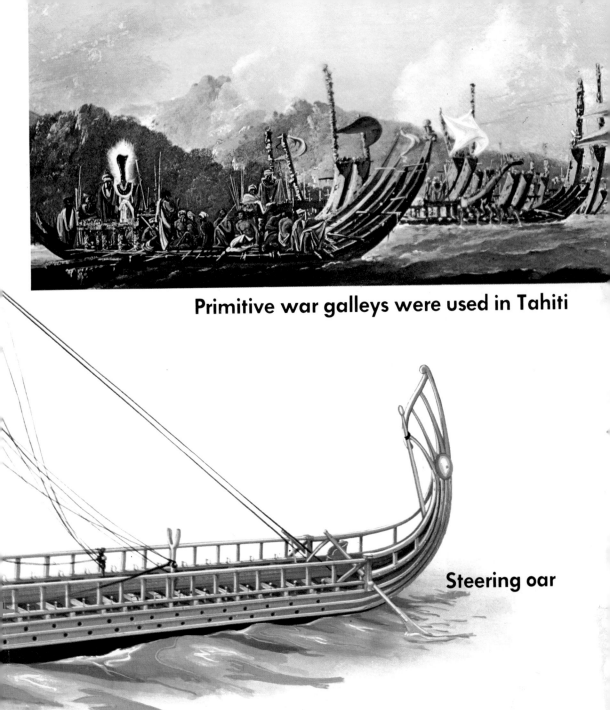

Primitive war galleys were used in Tahiti

Steering oar

Oars, Paddles and Sails

The strange-looking warship below was used by the Chinese. The crew turned handles to work the paddle-wheels.

The Vikings made long narrow ships which could be sailed up shallow rivers.

Viking longship

Chinese paddle junk

Viking longships could also be rowed by oars. They carried about 50 warriors.

Warships in Northern Europe developed from the longship. They carried soldiers in small wooden 'castles' on bow and stern.

Early English sailing ship

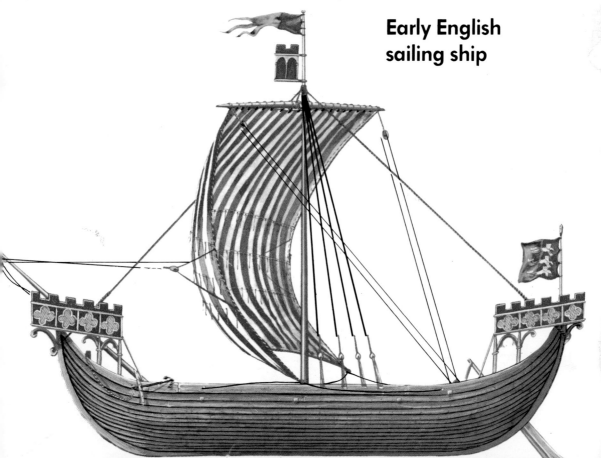

Warships with Guns

Early battles at sea were very similar to land battles. Two ships came alongside each other. Then, soldiers from one ship would try to board the other ship.

All this changed when cannons were put into warships.

Portuguese carrack
*Santa Catarina
do Monte Sinai*

Cannons made it easier to sink an enemy ship. Warships were no longer filled with soldiers. Instead, they had a crew of sailors.

The ship shown here is a carrack from the sixteenth century. She carried more than 160 cannons.

Fighting Sail

Many of the best sailing warships were built in Holland and Britain. These ships needed crews of hundreds of men to work them. Most jobs had to be done by men, not machines.

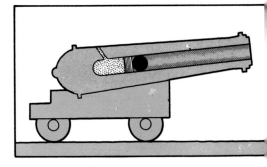

Interior of a cannon

Vasa, **Swedish warship of the 17th century**

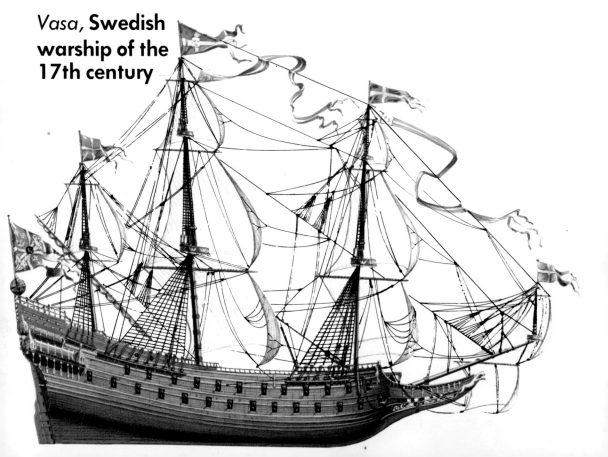

H.M.S. *Victory*

Different kinds of shot

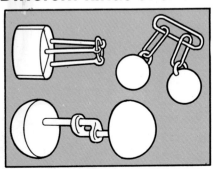

H.M.S. *Victory* is the best-known British fighting ship of all. She carried a crew of 850 men. Many looked after the sails and rigging. They often had to climb up the swaying masts in high winds.

The Age of Steam

Among the first armour-plated warships were these two 'Ironclads' (right). They fought in the American Civil War. They were steam-driven.

For several years, however, most steamships also carried sails (below).

H.M.S. *Agincourt*

H.M.S. *Dreadnought*

The first of the giant modern battleships was called H.M.S. *Dreadnought*. She had no sails, and was driven by steam. She carried powerful guns. Many countries built ships which copied the *Dreadnought*.

World War Two

The ships all travelling together are called a convoy. Some are oil tankers. Others are merchant ships carrying supplies or troops. Warships try to protect the convoy from enemy attack.

German battleship *Bismarck*

Aircraft were faster and had better guns than the planes of World War 1. The British battleship *Prince of Wales* was sunk in the South China Sea by Japanese aircraft, using bombs and torpedoes.

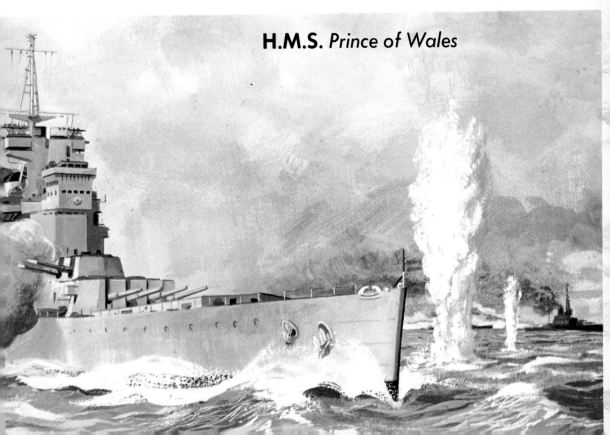

H.M.S. *Prince of Wales*

Modern nuclear submarine (cutaway)

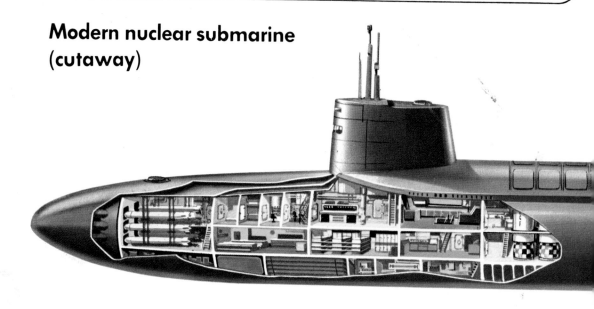

Submarines are warships that can travel under water. In the early submarines there was not much space for the crew. A lot of space was needed for diesel fuel. When the submarine travelled under water, it was powered by electric batteries.

Submarines can sink enemy ships by firing torpedoes at them.

EARLY SUBMARINES

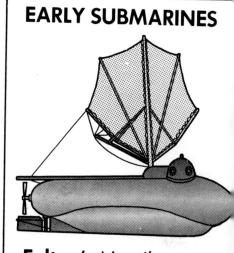

Fulton's *Nautilus* **(British) 1800**

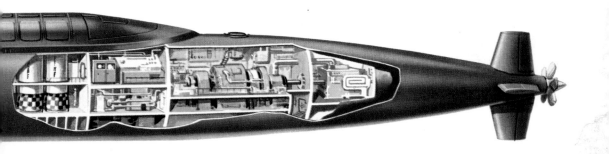

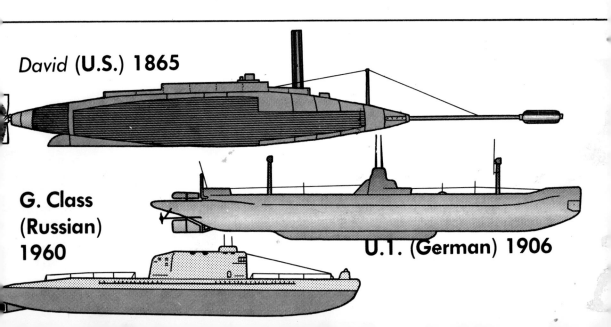

David (**U.S.**) **1865**

G. Class (Russian) 1960

U.1. (German) 1906

Aircraft Carriers

This huge ship is an aircraft carrier. Aircraft carriers are really floating runways. They carry aircraft inside their hull. The aircraft are brought up to the flight deck on huge lifts. When a plane takes off, a giant catapult helps it on its way.

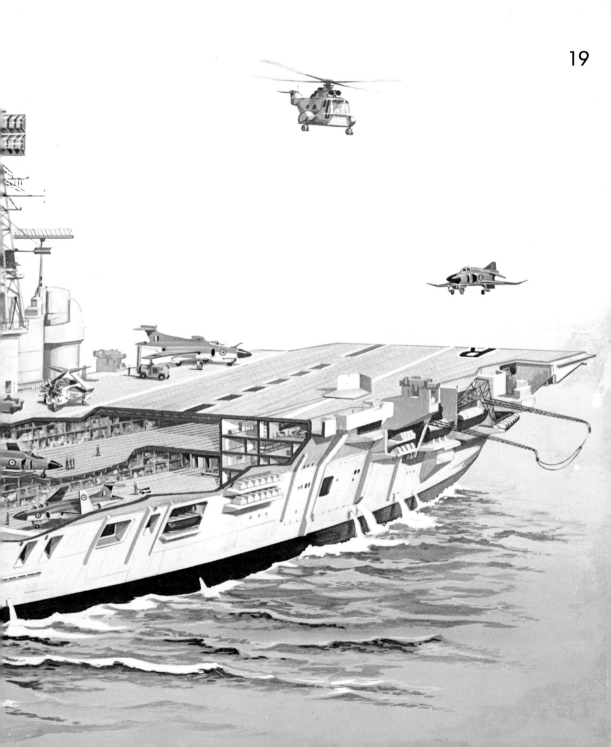

Battleships and aircraft carriers have become too expensive for most countries. They are also easy targets for modern weapons.

Today, warships are often armed with missiles (rockets) instead of guns.

Many modern navies use hovercraft, like the one below.

Hydrofoil

Hovercraft

The U.S. navy uses hovercraft and hydrofoils. At full speed the hull of a hydrofoil lifts clear of the water.

One of the new ideas in the British navy is the 'through-deck' cruiser (below). It will be able to do many different jobs, including carrying aircraft.

'Through-deck' cruiser

Battleship   The largest kind of warship.

Bow   The front part of a ship.

Cannon   An old type of large, heavy gun.

Carrack   A large merchant sailing ship of the Middle Ages.

Crew   A group of seamen looking after a ship.

Deck   The floor of a ship. There are usually several decks on different levels.

Galley   A long, low ship, driven by sails and oars.

Hovercraft   A vehicle which skims the surface of the water, riding on a cushion of air.

Hull   The outer framework of a ship.

Hydrofoil   A boat whose hull lifts out of the water to increase its speed.

Paddle-wheel   A large wheel with 'fins' that was used on some ships to drive them through the water.

Ram   A strong 'beak' at the front of a warship for smashing into an enemy ship.

Rigging   Ropes and pulleys that support the masts of a ship and move the sails.

Stern   The back part of a ship.

Torpedoes   Cigar-shaped weapons carrying explosives. They are used to attack enemy ships below the waterline.

2 3 4 5 6 7 8 9 10— R —85 84 83 82